On The Farm

Colouring Books

GW01191314

Day One

"I myself
will tend my
sheep"
Ezekiel 34:15

"Let the land produce living creatures"
Genesis 1:24

the sty

"Love each other as I have loved you."
John 15:12

"The creatures of the field are mine."
Psalm 50:11

"My sheep listen to my voice; I know them, and they follow me."
John 10:27

"See how the farmer waits for the land to yield its valuable crop"

James 5:7

"Do you give the horse his strength?"
Job 39:19

"A farmer went out to sow his seed." Luke 8:5

Better a meal
of vegetables
where there
is love
Proverbs 15:17

The Rainbow Colouring Book Range...

Creation

Christmas

Harvest

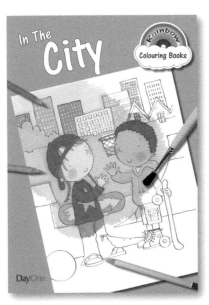

In the City

In the Country

On the Beach

Available from Day One

Rainbow Colouring Books

On the Farm

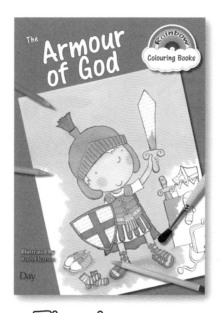

The Armour
of God

Children
in the Bible

Colours
in the Bible

Food
in the Bible

© **Day One Publications** 2011
Reprinted 2019

ISBN 978-1-84625-302-7

Scripture quotations are from The New International Version

Published by Day One Publications
Ryelands Road, Leominster, HR6 8NZ
sales@dayone.co.uk | www.dayone.co.uk
Tel: +44 (0) 1568 613 740
Tel Toll Free: 888 329 6630 (North America)

All rights reserved

No part of this publication may be reproduced, or stored in a retrieval system, or transmitted, in any
form or by any means, mechanical, electronic, photocopying, recording or otherwise, without the prior
permission of Day One Publications.

Limited and specific waiver of copyright

Notwithstanding the notice above, however, permission is granted to your church, youth group, school
or similar organization to make use of the activities of these pages for fair and limited own use by
photocopying or similar copy method, provided such copies are not intended for resale or for use outside
of your church, youth group, school or similar organization.

Illustrations: Ruth Hearson   **Design:** Rob Jones

Printed by Orchard Press Cheltenham Ltd